Ella

ALAN MACDONALD

Illustrated by Beccy Blake

OXFORD
UNIVERSITY PRESS

OXFORD
UNIVERSITY PRESS

Great Clarendon Street, Oxford OX2 6DP

Oxford University Press is a department of the University of Oxford.
It furthers the University's objective of excellence in research, scholarship,
and education by publishing worldwide in

Oxford   New York
Auckland   Cape Town   Dar es Salaam   Hong Kong   Karachi
Kuala Lumpur   Madrid   Melbourne   Mexico City   Nairobi
New Delhi   Shanghai   Taipei   Toronto

With offices in
Argentina   Austria   Brazil   Chile   Czech Republic   France   Greece
Guatemala   Hungary   Italy   Japan   Poland   Portugal   Singapore
South Korea   Switzerland   Thailand   Turkey   Ukraine   Vietnam

Oxford is a registered trade mark of Oxford University Press
in the UK and in certain other countries

Text © Alan MacDonald 2006

British Library Cataloguing in Publication Data
Data available

ISBN 978-0-19-911336-1

9 10 8

Available in packs
Stage 9 Pack of 6:
ISBN 978-0-19-911333-0
Stage 9 Class Pack:
ISBN 978-0-19-911334-7
Guided Reading Cards also available:
ISBN 978-0-19-911341-5

Printed in China by Imago

1

Come to my party

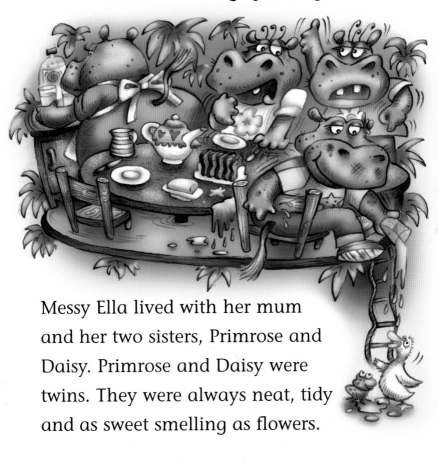

Messy Ella lived with her mum
and her two sisters, Primrose and
Daisy. Primrose and Daisy were
twins. They were always neat, tidy
and as sweet smelling as flowers.

Messy Ella wasn't neat or tidy. She was a mucky, muddy kind of hippo.

One day a letter arrived at Messy Ella's house. It was an invitation.

Please come to my Garden Party
Tonight!
6pm–9pm
At Pottingham Palace

Prince Potsy

Messy Ella showed the invitation to her sisters.

They grabbed it at once.

'A garden party! What fun!'
Primrose said. 'There'll be lots of
yummy food…'

'And ballroom dancing,' Daisy said.
'I bet Prince Potsy will dance with me.'

'No, he won't. He'll dance with *me*,'
Primrose snorted.

'Can I go?' Messy Ella asked.

'Oh, no!' Primrose said. 'You're much too messy.'

Messy Ella looked at herself. She *was* a bit of a mess. She'd been making mud pies in the garden.

But she loved parties, so she went to find her mum.

'Please can I go to the party, Mum?' Messy Ella begged.

'P-l-e-a-s-e?'

She kept on… and on… until at last her mother gave in.

'But you *must* look clean and tidy!' her mum warned.

Messy Ella was so excited she ran upstairs and put on her party dress.

2

'We'll look after you'

'Oh, Messy Ella! Don't wear that dress now,' said her mum. 'You'll get it dirty.'

'I won't, Mum,' Messy Ella promised. 'I'll be *very* careful.'

'All right,' her mum sighed. 'But if you spoil that dress, you can't go to the party.'

Messy Ella sat on the sofa. She didn't move. She wanted to run and play but she didn't dare get her dress dirty.

Primrose and Daisy smiled at one another.

'Come outside with us,' Daisy said.

'But what about my dress?' Messy Ella said. 'I'll get it dirty.'

'We'll look after you,' Daisy smiled.

'Okay,' said Messy Ella. 'I'm bored of sitting here.'

Primrose and Daisy took Messy Ella
down the road. There were lots of
muddy puddles.

'Messy Ella, I bet you couldn't jump
over that puddle,' said Primrose.

'I could!' said Messy Ella. 'I'm good
at jumping!'

She tried to jump over it.

'See!' said Messy Ella. 'I *told* you I could do it.'

'Oh, Messy Ella, you *are* clever!' smiled her sisters.

SPLAT!

Then they came to a prickly hedge.

'Messy Ella, I bet you couldn't crawl through that hole in the hedge,' said Daisy.

'I bet I could!' said Messy Ella. 'I'm good at crawling through holes.'

At first she got stuck, but the twins pushed and Messy Ella crawled through the hedge.

'Oh Messy Ella, you *are* brave!' sniggered Primrose and Daisy.

Then they came to a stream and Daisy spotted a rope swing.

'I bet you couldn't swing across the stream on that rope,' said Daisy.

'I *could*,' said Messy Ella. 'I'm good at swinging on ropes.'

Messy Ella held onto the rope and her sisters gave her a big push.

She almost made it across… almost, but not quite.

'Oh, dear!' said Messy Ella.

'You *are* a mess!' Primrose giggled.

When Messy Ella got home, her dress was muddy, torn and dripping wet. Her mum was very cross.

'Look at you!' she stormed. 'Your dress is *ruined!* Now you'll have to stay at home and miss the party.'

3

Swish! Swoosh!

Messy Ella begged and begged but it
was no good. At six o'clock her sisters
went off to the party without her.

'Bye-bye, Messy Ella! We'll tell you
all about it tomorrow,' they giggled.

Messy Ella went up to her room
in tears.

She lay on her bed and cried
and cried.

She really wanted to go to the party.
She really wanted to see Pottingham
Palace and meet Prince Potsy.

'It's not fair,' she sobbed. 'I *wish* I
could go!'

There was a puff of pink smoke.

A kind old hippo stood smiling
at her.

'Who... who are you?' Messy Ella
sniffed.

'I am your Fairy Godmother,' said
the old hippo. 'Why are you crying?'

Messy Ella explained about her
sisters and how she had ruined her
dress. The Fairy Godmother listened.

Then she waved her wand.

'Messy Ella,' she said, 'you *shall* go to the party!'

Messy Ella looked down at her clothes.

Her torn, muddy dress had vanished. Now she was wearing a sparkly tee shirt and jeans!

'Wow!' said Messy Ella. 'I look great! But how can I get to the party? I'm late already.'

The Fairy Godmother waved her wand again.

Messy Ella's muddy trainers turned into silver roller blades.

'Oh, *thank you*, Fairy Godmother!' cried Messy Ella. She whizzed off down the road at top speed.

4

'Who's *that*?'

Messy Ella arrived at Pottingham
Palace. She zoomed in on her roller
blades and skidded to a halt.

All the other hippos stared at her.
Prince Potsy stared most of all.

'Who's *that*?' Primrose whispered
to Daisy.

'I don't know,' Daisy said. 'She looks a bit like our messy little sister.'

'Don't be silly!' Primrose said. 'She's *much* too pretty. Anyway, Messy Ella's at home.'

Prince Potsy leaped on to the table.

'Okay, everyone, it's time to play some games!' he shouted.

'Games?' said Primrose. 'I don't *like* games!'

'And what about the ballroom dancing?' asked Daisy.

But the prince wasn't interested in ballroom dancing.

He wanted to play jumping games... and crawling-through-holes games...

…and swinging-on-ropes games.

Primrose and Daisy didn't want to join in, but they were the only ones who weren't playing. In the end, they had to.

But they weren't good at games like Messy Ella.

They got splashed jumping in the puddles. They tore their dresses crawling through the holes.

When they swung on the ropes, they fell off every time.

Prince Potsy didn't even notice them. He only wanted to be with one person – the mysterious hippo on the silver roller blades.

Messy Ella had a wonderful time.

Then the clock struck nine. Messy Ella said goodbye to the prince and whizzed home.

She crept into bed before her mum came up to say goodnight.

Primrose and Daisy weren't so lucky.
Their mum met them at the door.

'Look at your party dresses!' she
gasped. 'They're ruined! *Ruined!*'

They were sent straight to bed.
Messy Ella was waiting for them.

'How was the party?' she asked.

'Wonderful,' Primrose said, telling a big lie.

'Prince Potsy danced with me all night,' Daisy added.

'Really?' Messy Ella smiled.

Primrose and Daisy didn't answer. They were staring at the silver roller blades at the end of Messy Ella's bed.

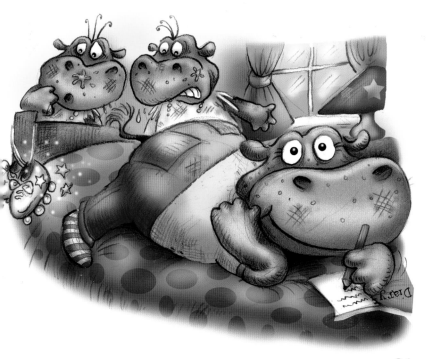

About the author

I live in Nottingham and
write books for children
and scripts for TV.

I've always enjoyed folk
tales and fairy stories.
Messy Ella is of course based
on Cinderella. But in this
story I didn't want a heroine who
was sweet as cherry pie. Ella is mucky
and messy, so keeping her party dress
clean for a whole day is asking the
impossible. From that beginning the
story began to grow.